D0594484

Moving Forward, Keeping Still

The Gateway to
Eastern Wisdom

BARNES
&NOBLE
BOOKS
NEW YORK

Published by MJF Books
Fine Communications
322 Eighth Avenue
New York, NY 10001

Moving Forward, Keeping Still
LC Control Number 2002117560
ISBN 1-56731-609-3

Manufactured in the United States of America on acid-free paper ∞

MJF Books and the MJF colophon are trademarks of Fine Creative
Media, Inc.

VB   10   9   8   7   6   5   4   3   2

Moving
Forward,
Keeping
Still

INTRODUCTION

Once the whole is divided,
the parts need names.
There are already enough names.

—TAO TE CHING

Names can be very powerful. In the ancient world it was believed that knowing the name of an enemy gave one power over him. From names we

7

build facts and figures; mathematical equations; theories, concepts, and systems. The technological achievements of the West have proven well the power of this kind of thinking. Yet there remains the feeling of incompleteness. We try harder, examining the world and ourselves even more closely, resulting in more names. But it is easy to fall into the trap of thinking that merely by naming something we come to understand it.

When we sift, analyze, classify, and break down everything into pieces, we are left with just that—pieces. Reality cannot be reduced to bite-size chunks; it must be swallowed whole. Grand, universal systems of science and philosophy are equally dissatisfying as a pile of pieces: They strip each thing and moment of its uniqueness, leaving behind abstractions rather than the things themselves.

The traditional wisdom of the East provides a different path and a different view: Reality is larger than any container we can devise, whether it be language, mathematics, or religion. Since reality encompasses both the general and specific—the whole as well as the pieces—Eastern thought embraces these opposites and permits the contradictions. Thus, opposites do not merely oppose, they complement each other. Light and dark, high and low, sound and silence are mutually defining, in that it is impossible to describe one without recourse to the other. And together they make up a whole greater than the sum of the parts.

Much of the traditional religious practice of the East involves giving up preconception and seeing things as they are, rather than what we would like them to be. This book brings together sayings and quotations from that Eastern tradition. You may find them to be poetic, surprising, baffling, even humorous—but upon repeated reading and reflection, you may find yourself less concerned with classifying, less worried about naming. As a result, you may see more. You may find yourself asking, like the Chinese philosopher Chuang Tzu, "Where can I find a man who has forgotten the words? He is the one I would like to talk to."

11

When you are deluded and full of doubt, even a thousand books of scripture are not enough.

When you have realized understanding, even one word is too much.

FEN-YANG

13

The bird that cries korokoro in the mountain rice-field I know to be a hototogisu—yet it may have been my father; it may have been my mother.

JAPANESE BUDDHIST
PROVERB

We shape clay into
a pot, but it is the
emptiness inside that
holds whatever we want.

Tao te Ching

I am the vessel.
The draught is God's.
And God is the
thirsty one.

Dag Hammarskjöld

16

Keep your hands open, and all the sands of the desert can pass through them. Close them, and all you can feel is a bit of grit.

TAISEN DESHIMARU

17

Those in a hurry
do not arrive.

Zen saying

18

Emperor: "What happens to the man of
   enlightenment and the man of illusion
   after death?"
Zen master: "How should I know, sir?"
Emperor: "Because you're a master!"
Zen master: "Yes, but no dead one, sir!"

GUDO

Absence of
evidence is not
evidence of absence.

Anonymous

20

The steadfast
go out like
this lamp.

Suttanipata

21

Better than the one
who knows what is
right is he who loves
what is right.

Confucius

Monk: "I have just entered the monastery: please give me some guidance."
Master: "Have you eaten your rice gruel?"
Monk: "Yes, I've eaten."
Master: "Then go wash your bowl."

ZEN *MONDO*

No object is
mysterious. The
mystery is your eye.

Elizabeth Bowen

24

The superior man
seeks what is right;
the inferior one,
what is profitable.

Confucius

25

A master who
cannot bow to his
disciple cannot
bow to Buddha.

Shunryu Suzuki

Those who seek the truth by means of intellect and learning only get further and further away from it. Not till your thoughts cease all their branching here and there, not till you abandon all thoughts of seeking for something, not till your mind is motionless as wood or stone, will you be on the right road to the Gate.

HUANG PO

Cut down the
whole forest
of desire, not just
one tree only.

Dhammapada

The mind is everything;
what you think,
you become.

Buddha

29

The need is not to
amputate the ego
but to transcend it.

Norman Cousins

30

Formerly, when religion was strong and science weak, men mistook magic for medicine; now, when science is strong and religion weak, men mistake medicine for magic.

THOMAS SZASZ

31

Aspecial transmission outside the
Scriptures;
No dependence upon words and letters;
Direct pointing to reality;
Seeing into one's own nature and realizing
Buddhahood.

BODHIDHARMA

Rather than spend
aeons without an
awakening, have
no second thoughts.

Jakushitsu

33

The whole of existence
is imagination within
imagination, while true
Being is God alone.

Ibn ' Arabi

34

God has no religion.

Gandhi

35

It took me four years
to paint like Raphael,
but a lifetime to paint
like a child.

Pablo Picasso

Atop a hundred-foot
pole, how do you
step forward?

Shishuang

37

Let not the fruit of action be your motive to action. Your business is with action alone, not with the fruit of action.

BHAGAVAD GITA

Hatred is never appeased by hatred in this world; it is appeased by love. This is an eternal Law.

DHAMMAPADA

We must openly accept all ideologies and systems as means of solving humanity's problems. One country, one nation, one ideology, one system is not sufficient.

DALAI LAMA

Fear is the
absence of faith.

Paul Tillich

41

Zen has no
business with ideas.

D. T. Suzuki

But the Buddha also performed miracles. For example this one, a miracle of courtesy: The Buddha has to cross a desert at noon. The gods, from their thirty-three heavens, each send him down a parasol. The Buddha does not want to slight any of the gods, so he turns himself into thirty-three Buddhas. Each god sees a Buddha protected by the parasol he sent.

JORGE LUIS BORGES

Lighthouses are more
helpful than churches.

Benjamin Franklin

Our theories of the eternal are as valuable as are those that a chick which has not broken its way through its shell might form of the outside world.

BUDDHA

Healing only comes from that which leads the patient beyond himself and beyond his entanglements with ego.

C. G. JUNG

Unless we agree to
suffer we cannot be free
from suffering.

D. T. Suzuki

47

When you get there, there isn't any there there.

Gertrude Stein

48

The stopping of becoming is Nirvana.

Samyutta-nikaya II

49

After silence, that
which comes nearest
to expressing the
inexpressible is music.

Aldous Huxley

No trace: When you do something, you should burn yourself completely, like a good bonfire, leaving no trace of yourself.

SHUNRYU SUZUKI

W hile walking,
examine the walking;
while sitting,
the sitting. . . .

Zen saying

The notes I handle no better than many pianists. But the pauses between the notes—ah, that is where the art resides.

ARTUR SCHNABEL

I am trying to be
unfamiliar with
what I am doing.

John Cage

Chance implies an absolute absence of any principle.

Chuang Tzu

A little wisdom is a stumbling block on the way to Buddhahood.

Japanese Buddhist proverb

We work to become,

not to acquire.

Elbert Hubbard

The quieter you become,
the more you can hear.

Baba Ram Dass

Being is born
of not being.

Tao te Ching

The bird of paradise
alights only upon
the hand that
does not grasp.

John Berry

In a world of fugitives
The person taking the opposite direction
Will appear to run away.

T. S. ELIOT

61

We should take care not to make the intellect our god; it has, of course, powerful muscles, but no personality.

ALBERT EINSTEIN

I neither follow the Way nor depart from it. I neither worship the Buddha nor have contempt for him. I neither sit long hours in meditation nor sit idle. I neither eat just one meal a day nor am I greedy for more. I desire nothing, and that is what I call the Way.

VASUBANDHU

We must learn to
be still in the midst of
activity and to be
vibrantly alive in repose.

Indira Gandhi

Not collecting
treasures prevents
stealing.

Tao te Ching

The Kingdom of
Heaven is not a place,
but a state of mind.

John Burroughs

66

If your philosophy
doesn't grow corn,
I don't want to
hear about it.

Sun Bear

There is no ice or snow apart from water. The Buddhahood of ordinary people can be likened to snow and ice melting and becoming water. From the beginning nothing has ever been lost.

BASSUI

No snowflake
ever falls in the
wrong place.

Zen saying

Sin is energy in
the wrong channel.

Saint Augustine

70

Not nakedness, not matted locks, not dirt or fasting or sleeping on the bare earth, or sitting motionless can purify a man who has not overcome his doubts.

DHAMMAPADA

Not to have any
desire whatsoever—
that is the Way.

Keizan

72

There are children playing in the street who could solve some of my top problems in physics, because they have modes of sensory perception that I lost long ago.

J. ROBERT OPPENHEIMER

In walking, just walk.
In sitting, just sit.
Above all, don't wobble.

Yunmen

74

A great tailor
cuts little.

Tao te Ching

Better to see the
face than to hear
the name.

Zen saying

Wherever there is attachment
Association with it
Brings endless misery.

GAMPOPA

To be surprised,
to wonder, is to
begin to understand.

José Ortega y Gasset

Few among men are they who cross over to the further shore. The others merely run up and down the bank on this side.

DHAMMAPADA

Ahuman life is like a single letter in the alphabet. It can be meaningless. Or it can be part of a great meaning.

JEWISH THEOLOGICAL
SEMINARY OF AMERICA

80

However fickle I seem, my heart
is never unfaithful:
Out of the slime itself, spotless the
lotus grows.

JAPANESE FOLK SONG

The mind
should be nowhere
in particular.

Takuan

As is the atom,
so is the universe.

Upanishads

Zen cannot be defined. It is not a "thing" to be surrounded or reflected by words. When the last word is troweled into the prison it escapes and laughs away on the horizon.

DAVID BRANDON

All the way to heaven is heaven.

Saint Catherine of Siena

85

Self is the only
prison that can
ever bind the soul.

Henry Van Dyke

He who
grasps loses.

Tao te Ching

We cannot

get grace

from gadgets.

J. B. Priestley

The fool who knows
his foolishness is wise
to that extent.

Dhammapada

If you meet
the Buddha,
kill the Buddha.

Linji

Themselves the Zen expression "Kill the Buddha"
means to kill any concept of the Buddha
as something apart from yourself. To kill
the Buddha is to be the Buddha.

PETER MATTHIESSEN

One who knows
the Self puts
death to death.

Upanishads

The purpose of words is to convey ideas. When the ideas are grasped, the words are forgotten.

Where can I find a man who has forgotten the words? He is the one I would like to talk to.

CHUANG TZU

A good traveler
leaves no track.

Tao te Ching

The real voyage of discovery consists not in seeking new landscapes, but in having new eyes.

MARCEL PROUST

95

Even our enemy is useful to us because, in order to practice compassion we need to practice tolerance, forgiveness, and patience, the antidotes to anger.

DALAI LAMA

Whatever harm a foe may do to a foe, or a hater to another hater, a wrongly directed mind may do one harm far exceeding these.

DHAMMAPADA

97

Perfect happiness
is the absence
of happiness.

CHUANG TZU

As soon as you
have made a thought,
laugh at it.

Lao Tzu

Imagination is more
important than
knowledge.

Albert Einstein

100

What is meant ... by the term "illusion" is that phenomena do not exist independently of other phenomena, that their appearance of independent existence is illusory. This is all that is meant by "illusion," not that something is not really there.

DALAI LAMA

If a pickpocket
meets a Holy Man,
he will see only
his pockets.

Hari Dass

There are no
pockets in a shroud.

Church bulletin board

103

Things don't change.
You change your way
of looking, that's all.

Carlos Castaneda

We tend to wear suits of armor,
one over the other.... We hope we will
not have to completely undress.

CHÖGYAM TRUNGPA

If there is to be
any peace it will
come through being,
not having.

Henry Miller

Never let go
the reins of the
wild colt of the heart.

Japanese Buddhist proverb

107

Zen is consciousness unstructured by particular form or particular system, a transcultural, transreligious, transformed consciousness.

THOMAS MERTON

The map is not
the territory.

ALFRED KORZYBSKI

Reading about
enlightenment is
like scratching an itch
through your shoe.

Roshi Philip Kapleau

The Ultimate Path
is without difficulty;
Just avoid picking
and choosing.

The Blue Cliff Record

We should find
perfect existence through
imperfect existence.

Shunryu Suzuki

What time would it be if all the clocks were stopped?

Zen question

Thus is myself and this is another."
Be free of this bond which encompasses
  you about,
And your own self is thereby released

SARAHA'S TREASURY
OF SONGS

Fundamentally the
marksman aims
at himself.

*Zen in the Art
of Archery*

The mind is host,
the body guest.

Japanese saying

116

How old would you be if you didn't know how old you was?

Satchel Paige

117

An integral being knows without going, sees without looking, and accomplishes without doing.

LAO TZU

Mere suffering exists,
but no sufferer is found;
The deeds are, but
no doer is found.

Buddhaghosa

119

We now come to the very heart of Zen, which is, it might be said, to commit spiritual suicide.

KENNETH KRAMER

The sculptor produces the beautiful statue by chipping away such parts of the marble block as are not needed—it is a process of elimination.

ELBERT HUBBARD

121

The nature of God is a circle of
which the center is everywhere and
the circumference is nowhere.

EMPEDOCLES

There must be more
to life than having
everything!

Maurice Sendak

123

Even as a solid rock is unshaken by the wind, so are the wise unshaken by praise or blame.

DHAMMAPADA

Though it has no thought of keeping watch, it's not for naught that the scarecrow stands in the grain field.

DÔGEN ZENJI

There is nothing in
all creation so like
God as stillness.

Meister Eckhart

126

Come, behold this world, how it resembles an ornamented chariot, in which fools flounder, but for the wise there is no attachment to it.

DHAMMAPADA

127

Mischief all comes
from much opening
of the mouth.

Chinese proverb

There is only the one reality, neither to be realized or attained. To say "I am able to realize something" or "I am able to attain something" is to place yourself among the arrogant.

HUANG PO

Attention comes from nowhere. It has no cause. It belongs to no one. When it functions effortlessly, there is no duality.

TONI PACKER

130

In the cultivation of the mind, our emphasis should be not on concentration, but on attention. Concentration is a process of forcing the mind to narrow down to a point, whereas attention is without frontiers.

J. KRISHNAMURTI

131

Why seek a doctrine?
As soon as you have a
doctrine, you fall into
dualistic thought.

Huang Po

Once the self
does not exist,
How could
the *mine* exist?

Nagarjuna

133

In the early days of the Indian Territory, there were no such things as birth certificates. You being there was certificate enough.

WILL ROGERS

The greatest prayer
is patience.

Buddha

135

My karma ran
over my dogma.

Bumper sticker

If you don't believe
in the gods,
leave them alone.

Chinese proverb

The ultimate standpoint of Zen ... is that we have been led astray through ignorance to find a split in our own being, that there was from the very beginning no need for a struggle between the finite and the infinite, that the peace we are seeking so eagerly has been there all the time.

D. T. SUZUKI

Victory breeds hatred. He who has given up both victory and defeat, he is contented and happy.

DHAMMAPADA

139

Do not seek the truth. Only cease to cherish opinions.

Zen saying

140

The world is so constructed, that if you wish to enjoy its pleasures, you also must endure its pains.

SWAMI BRAHMANANDA

There are three kinds of disciples: those who impart Zen to others, those who maintain the temples and shrines, and then there are the rice bags and the clothes hangers.

NYOGEN SENZAKI

Whoever shall exalt himself shall be abased; and he that shall humble himself shall be exalted.

MATTHEW 23:12

No matter what
road I travel,
I'm going home.

Shinso

To know the
road ahead, ask
those coming back.

Chinese proverb

There is no place
to seek the mind;
It is like the footprints
of birds in the sky.

Zenrin

146

Monk: "What is the most valuable thing in this world?"

Master: "A dead cat."

Monk: "Why?"

Master: "Because no one can put a price on it."

ZEN *MONDO*

Not only can I not recall my experiences in my previous lives, sometimes I can't even remember what I did yesterday.

DALAI LAMA

W

ork is prayer.

Work is also stink.

Therefore stink is prayer.

Aldous Huxley

149

Don't play what's there, play what's not there.

Miles Davis

Nirvana may be the final object of attainment, but at the moment, it is difficult to reach. Thus, the practical and realistic aim is compassion, a warm heart, serving other people, helping others, respecting others, being less selfish.

DALAI LAMA

Outside noisy,
inside empty.

Chinese proverb

We can think of the
soul not as an entity
but as a principle.

D. T. Suzuki

Ultimately, the
only healthy person
is a Buddha.

Dalai Lama

All living beings hate pain; therefore one should not injure them or kill them. This is the essence of wisdom: not to kill anything.

SUTRA-KRIT-ANGA

Sitting quietly,
doing nothing,
Spring comes and
the grass grows by itself.

Zenrin

156

The universe is
a single life
comprising one
substance and one soul.

Marcus Aurelius

The game is not about becoming somebody, it's about becoming nobody.

Baba Ram Dass

He who knows
he has enough
is rich.

Tao te Ching

We are to practice
virtue, not possess it.

Meister Eckhart

160

Knowledge is one. Its division into subjects is a concession to human weakness.

SIR HALFORD
JOHN MACKINDER

*D*e lo que veas cree muy poco,
De lo que te cuenten, nada.

[Of that which you see, believe only
    a little,
Of that which you are told, nothing.]

Blow and you can
extinguish a fire.
Blow and you can
make a fire.

Zen koan

163

*K*eine *A*ntwort ist

auch eine *A*ntwort.

[No answer is also an answer.]

German proverb

164

The fewer words
the better prayer.

Martin Luther

There is no place
to which we could
flee from God which
is outside God.

Paul Tillich

166

What will it profit
a man if he should
gain the whole world,
if he loses his own soul?

Matthew 16:26

The greatest form
has no shape.

Lao Tzu

We have to move
from the illusion
of certainty to the
certainty of illusion.

Sam Keen

169

Both speech and
silence transgress.

Zen saying

As far as the laws of mathematics refer to reality, they are not certain; as far as they are not certain, they do not refer to reality.

ALBERT EINSTEIN

The reverse side
has also its
reverse side.

Japanese proverb

172

Man's heart is like a printing block. If the block does not err, then even if one copies ten million papers, there will not be errors. If the block errs, then if one repeatedly copies them on paper there will be none without errors.

WANG HSUN

There is no
enlightenment
outside of daily life.

Thich Nhat Hanh

174

Only the supremely wise and the abysmally ignorant do not change.

Confucius

175

Hope and fear cannot alter the seasons.

Chögyam Trungpa

Power of mind
is infinite while
brawn is limited.

Koichi Tohei

177

What we call "I" is just a swinging door which moves when we inhale and exhale.

SHUNRYU SUZUKI

He who carves the
Buddha never
worships him.

Chinese proverb

179

Gaining enlightenment is like the moon reflected on the water. The moon doesn't get wet; the water isn't broken. Although its light is broad and great, the moon is reflected even in a puddle an inch wide. The whole moon and the whole sky are reflected in one dewdrop on the grass.

DÔGEN ZENJI

If you shut your door
to all errors
truth will be shut out.

Rabindranath Tagore

181

We think in
generalities, but we
live in detail.

Alfred North Whitehead

182

To have some deep feeling about Buddhism is not the point; we just do what we should do, like eating supper and going to bed. This is Buddhism.

SHUNRYU SUZUKI

183

Flow with whatever may happen and let your mind be free: Stay centered by accepting whatever you are doing. This is the ultimate.

CHUANG TZU

Make a hairbreadth difference, and Heaven and Earth are set apart.

Seng-tsan

One cannot
step twice into
the same river.

Heracleitus

To know and
to act are one
and the same.

Samurai maxim

187

W hat happens to
the hole when
the cheese is gone?

Bertolt Brecht

The universe is
made up of stories,
not atoms.

Muriel Rukeyser

189

In every speck of
dust are Buddhas
without number.

Anonymous

My true desire is
to relieve others of their
pain though I myself
may fall into hell.

Bassui

191

Zen is the
unsymbolization
of the world.

R. H. Blyth

It takes a very
long time to
become young.

Pablo Picasso

193

Do every act
of your life as if
it were your last.

Marcus Aurelius

194

Monk: "If I have nothing in my mind, what should I do?"

Master: "Throw it away."

Monk: "But how can I throw nothing away?"

Master: "Then carry it away."

ZEN *MONDO*

Memory is
incomplete
experience.

J. Krishnamurti

196

The nature of the Mind when
understood,
No human speech can compass or
disclose.

HUANG PO

There is a taint worse
than all taints, and its
name is ignorance.

Dhammapada

A language
is a map of
our failures.

Adrienne Rich

199

Life is like a game of cards. The hand that is dealt you represents determinism; the way you play it is free will.

JAWAHARLAL NEHRU

E,verything should
be as simple as it is,
but not simpler.

Albert Einstein

There's never been
a single thing;
Then where's defiling
dust to cling?

Hui Neng

202

W here there
is fear there is
no religion.

Gandhi

Those who come talking of right
    and wrong
Are therefore right and wrong people.

WUMEN

By your stumbling,
the world is perfected.

Sri Aurobindo

W

hen a dog
runs at you,
whistle for him.

Henry David Thoreau

206

If you will conceive
of a Buddha, *you
will be obstructed
by that Buddha!*

Huang Po

207

To see is to forget
the name of
the thing one sees.

Paul Valéry

208

When the clouds
fly the moon travels;
when a boat goes
the shore moves.

Buddha

209

Beware, as they say,
of mistaking the finger
for the moon when
you're pointing at it.

John Cage

Descartes said,
"I think, therefore I am."
I say, "I do not think,
that is why I exist."

Taisen Deshimaru

211

How can you think and hit at the same time?

Yogi Berra

The world is so wide,
so vast; why put on a
formal vestment at the
sound of a bell?

Yunmen

213

Quit this world.
Quit the next world.
Quit quitting.

Baba Ram Dass

The first sign of
your becoming religious
is that you are
becoming cheerful.

Swami Vivekananda

I can't hear
myself hearing.

Marcel Duchamp

Eternity is not something that happens after you are dead. It is going on all the time. We are in it now.

CHARLOTTE PERKINS
GILMAN

Muddy water,
let stand,
becomes clear.

Lao Tzu

218

To see the world in a grain of sand,
And a heaven in a wild flower,
Hold infinity in the palm of your hand
And eternity in an hour.

WILLIAM BLAKE

219

Later

never exists.

Anonymous

Heaven-sent calamities you may stand up against, but you cannot survive those brought on by yourself.

SHU CHING

Only the hand
that erases can write
the true thing.

Meister Eckhart

Before you attain it, it is something wonderful, but after you obtain it, it is nothing special.

SHUNRYU SUZUKI

Matter is less material and the mind less spiritual than is generally supposed. The habitual separation of physics and psychology, mind and matter, is metaphysically indefensible.

BERTRAND RUSSELL

A rose is a
rose is a rose.

Gertrude Stein

What is mind?
No matter. What is
matter? Never mind.

Thomas Hewitt Key

226

The raft of
knowledge ferries
the worst sinner
to safety.

Bhagavad Gita

227

Holding himself
good, one loses
one's goodness.

Shu Ching

228

Tolerance and patience should not be read as signs of weakness. They are signs of strength.

DALAI LAMA

229

It is as hard to see one's self as to look backwards without turning around.

Henry David Thoreau

One does not become enlightened by imagining figures of light, but by making the darkness conscious.

C. G. JUNG

That man alone is
wise who remains
master of himself.

Confucius

232

To embody the
transcendent is why
we are here.

Sogyal Rinpoche

The thing about Zen is that it pushes contradictions to their ultimate limit where one has to choose between madness and innocence.

THOMAS MERTON

234

If ordinary people know, they are sages; if sages understand, they are ordinary people.

WUMEN

235

The truth is that everything is One, and this of course is not a numerical one.

Roshi Philip Kapleau

236

Infinite worlds appear and disappear in the vast expanse of my own consciousness, like motes of dust dancing in a heaven of light.

ANCIENT VEDIC SAYING

I have taught that
when error ceases,
You know yourself
for what you are.

Saraha's Treasury of Songs

238

Monk: "What is mind?"
Master: "Mind."
Monk: "I do not understand."
Master: "Neither do I."

Zen *mondo*

If you are too
excited by joy,
later you will
have to cry.

Tibetan saying

240

Does the devil
know he is
a devil?

Elizabeth Madox Roberts

As a beautiful flower that is full of hue but lacks fragrance, even so fruitless is the well-spoken word of one who does not practice it.

DHAMMAPADA

Of the universal mind each individual man is one more incarnation.

Ralph Waldo Emerson

243

A man of
consummate activity
knows no rules
to follow.

Zen saying

244

Doctrine is nothing but the skin of truth, set up and stuffed.

Henry Ward Beecher

245

Do not think that
you can love God
and despise creation.
The two are at root One.

Rabbi Chanina

After attaining enlightenment, I want to save the bright and the dull, teaching each one according to his capacity.

BASSUI

Only the Supreme Executioner kills. To kill in place of the Supreme Executioner is to hack in place of a great carpenter. Now if one hacks in place of a great carpenter one can scarcely avoid cutting one's hand.

LAO TZU

Whether invoked
or not, God will
be present.

C. G. Jung

Throwing away Zen mind is correct Zen mind. Only keep the question, "What is the best way of helping other people?"

SEUNG SAHN

Men are suffering from the fever of violent emotion, and so they make a philosophy of it.

SARVEPALLI

RADHAKRISHNAN

251

The power of a man's virtue should be measured not by his special efforts, but by his ordinary doing.

BLAISE PASCAL

Go is in me
or else is
not at all.

Wallace Stevens

253

One day a student asked Ike no Taiga, "What is the most difficult part of painting?" Taiga said, "The part of the paper where nothing is painted is the most difficult."

ZEN PARABLE

No suffering
befalls the man
who calls nothing
his own.

Dhammapada

If you do not get
it from yourself,
Where will you
go for it?

Alan Watts

The bird in a forest can perch but
on one bough.
And this should be the wise man's
pattern.

TSO SSU

We take a handful of sand from the endless landscape of awareness around us and call that handful of sand the world.

ROBERT M. PIRSIG

When all discrimination is abandoned, when contact with things is broken, the mind is brighter than sun and moon together, cleaner than frost and snow.

ZEN PRAYER

Those who remember
that we must come to an
end in this world, their
quarrels cease at once.

Dhammapada

260

When one eye is fixed upon your destination, there is only one eye left with which to find the Way.

Meditation is not
the means to an end.
It is both the means
and the end.

J. Krishnamurti

Do not fear mistakes.
There are none.

Miles Davis

The great man is
sparing in words
but prodigal
in deeds.

Confucius

264

Foolish friends
are worse than
wise enemies.

Dhammapada

265

After the game,
the king and pawn
go into the same box.

Italian proverb

*S*eldom are fine
words and a studied
mien associated with
the right feeling.

Confucius

The wise man sets
no high value on a
thing simply because
it is hard to get.

Tao te Ching

Epigrams succeed
where epics fail.

Persian proverb

269

The greater the dignity of the angels in the celestial hierarchy, the fewer words they use; so that the most elevated of all pronounces only a single syllable.

IGOR STRAVINSKY

270

In quarreling about
the shadow, we often
lose the substance.

Aesop

271

Things derive their being and nature by mutual dependence and are nothing in themselves.

NAGARJUNA

The point we emphasize is strong confidence in our original nature.

Shunryu Suzuki

273

We do not want
churches because they
will teach us to
quarrel about God.

Chief Joseph

The Buddha and all his successors warn us against intellectual structures that confine us to an artificial environment, and against concepts that smear over the living fact of things in themselves.

ROBERT AITKEN

Control your emotion or it will control you.

Chinese proverb

276

The heart that breaks open can contain the whole universe.

Joanna Macy

For Zen

students a weed

is a treasure.

Shunryu Suzuki

278

In fact, it is dubious that one can even speak of "experiencing" reality, since this would imply a separation between the experiencer and the experience.

CHÖGYAM TRUNGPA

I never saw
a wild thing
sorry for itself.

D. H. Lawrence

280

One man cannot do right in one department of life whilst he is occupied in doing wrong in any other department. Life is one indivisible whole.

GANDHI

The peaches and
plums of the poor
houses also create shade.

Huguo

282

You carry
heaven and hell
with you.

Sri Ramana Maharshi

You must watch my life, how I live, eat, sit, talk, behave in general. The sum total of all those in me is my religion.

GANDHI

If your mind is empty, it is always ready for anything; it is open to everything. In the beginner's mind there are many possibilities; in the expert's mind there are few.

S H U N R Y U   S U Z U K I

Zen is joyous
iconoclasm which respects
nothing and no one,
particularly itself.

David Brandon

286

The angry man
will defeat himself
in battle as well
as in life.

Samurai maxim

The less effort,
the faster and
more powerful
you will be.

Bruce Lee

All that we are is the result of what we have thought: It is founded on our thoughts and is made up of our thoughts.

289

What science finds to be nonexistent, a Buddhist must necessarily accept, but what science merely does not find is a completely different matter. It is quite clear that there are many, many mysterious things.

DALAI LAMA

A little
unlearning goes
a long way.

Richard Kehl

Watchfulness is the path to immortality, and thoughtlessness the path to death. The watchful do not die, but the thoughtless are already like the dead.

Dhammapada

292

To ridicule
philosophy,
that is to be a
real philosopher.

Blaise Pascal

293

There is no
room for God
in him who is
full of himself.

Hasidic saying

294

Reality has
no inside, outside,
or middle part.

Bodhidharma

295

The epitome of the human realm is to be stuck in a huge traffic jam of discursive thought.

CHÖGYAM TRUNGPA

To know what we
do not know is the
beginning of wisdom.

*Maha Sthavira
Sangharakshita*

Inside yourself or outside, you never have to change what you see, only the way you see it.

Thaddeus Golas

To understand truth one must have a very sharp, precise, clear mind; not a cunning mind, but a mind that is capable of looking without any distortion, a mind innocent and vulnerable.

J. KRISHNAMURTI

299

If all beings
are Buddha, why
all this striving?

Dôgen Zenji

300

The no-mind
not-thinks
no-thoughts
about no-things.

Buddha

301

Die before
ye die.

Muhammad

302

A human being is part of the whole, called by us "the universe." Our task must be to widen our circle of compassion to embrace all living creatures and the whole of nature in its beauty.

ALBERT EINSTEIN

Among the most remarkable features characterizing Zen we find these: spirituality, directness of expression, disregard of form or conventionalism, and frequently an almost wanton delight in going astray from respectability.

D. T. SUZUKI

Since body and
mind are indivisible,
so are past and present.

Keizan

305

In order for a proposition to be capable of being true, it must also be capable of being false.

LUDWIG WITTGENSTEIN

If you don't know
how to serve men,
why worry about
serving the gods?

Confucius

The way of the
sage is to act but
not to compete.

Lao Tzu

308

The poet doesn't invent. He listens.

Jean Cocteau

Because each existence
is in constant change,
there is no abiding self.

Shunryu Suzuki

310

The intelligent man who is proud of his intelligence is like the condemned man who is proud of his large cell.

SIMONE WEIL

Think with the
whole body.

Taisen Deshimaru

One may conquer in battle a thousand times a thousand men, yet he is the best of conquerors who conquers himself.

DHAMMAPADA

313

A mind all logic
is like a knife all
blade. It makes the
hand bleed that uses it.

Rabindranath Tagore

314

We are not committed to this or that. We are committed to the nothing-in-between . . . whether we know it or not.

JOHN CAGE

Computers are useless. They can only give you answers.

Pablo Picasso

Thinking doesn't seem to help very much. The human brain is too high-powered to have many practical uses in this particular universe.

KURT VONNEGUT

317

Monk: "What does one think of while sitting?"
Master: "One thinks of not-thinking."
Monk: "How does one think of not-thinking?"
Master: "Without thinking."

ZEN MONDO

We can never have enough of that which we really do not want.

Eric Hoffer

319

We all want to be famous people, and the moment we want to *be* something we are no longer free.

J. KRISHNAMURTI

Dreams are real
while they last. Can
we say more of life?

Havelock Ellis

Trying to define
yourself is like
trying to bite
your own teeth.

Alan Watts

322

A tree that is
unbending is
easily broken.

Lao Tzu

A person who says, "I'm enlightened" probably isn't.

Baba Ram Dass

W hen you're green,
you're growing. When
you're ripe, you rot.

Ray Kroc

Master: "Do you smell the mountain laurel?"

Monk: "Yes."

Master: "There, I have held nothing back from you."

ZEN MONDO

One word of explanation already misses the mark.

Ejô

327

When they tell you
to grow up, they
mean stop growing.

Tom Robbins

328

If you think you're
free, there's no
escape possible.

Baba Ram Dass

Master: "As long as there is 'I and thou,' there is no seeing Tao."

Monk: "When there is neither 'I' nor 'thou' is it seen?"

Master: "When there is neither 'I' nor 'thou,' who is here to see it?"

ZEN *MONDO*

Preeminent scholars can obtain Tao in the battlefield. Secondary scholars can obtain Tao in urban areas. Lower scholars can obtain Tao only in the mountains.

PAO PIAO TSE

On the most exalted
throne in the world,
we are still seated on
nothing but our arse.

Michel de Montaigne

The evil life is
really the
thoughtless life.

Dhammapada

333

W hat is evil but
good tortured by its
own hunger and thirst?

Kahlil Gibran

334

Opinion has caused
more trouble on this
earth than all the
plagues and earthquakes.

Voltaire

A Zen master, when asked where he would go after he died, replied, "To hell, for that's where help is needed most."

ROSHI PHILIP KAPLEAU

336

Caught naked in an
unguarded moment,
Without past,
without future.

Dag Hammarskjöld

337

Forgetfulness of
self is remembrance
of God.

Bayazid al-Bistami

338

To live in fear and
falsehood is worse
than death.

Zend-Avesta

The ego, being a flimsy construction and being bound up in time and space, will have to fall apart. The ego, in fact, continuously falls apart and has to be reinforced by vanity, greed, jealousy and evil.

JANWILLEM
VAN DE WETERING

Often we find atheism both in individual and society a necessary passage to deeper religious and spiritual truth: One has sometimes to deny God in order to find Him.

SRI AUROBINDO

Usually when someone believes in a particular religion, his attitude becomes more and more a sharp angle pointing away from himself. In our way the point of the angle is always towards ourselves.

SHUNRYU SUZUKI

342

W hen the student
is ready, the
Master appears.

Japanese Buddhist proverb

343

To Zen, time and
eternity are one.

D. T. Suzuki

We can never really know. I simply believe that some part of the human Self or Soul is not subject to the laws of space and time.

C. G. JUNG

The next message
you need is right
where you are.

Baba Ram Dass

346

I really admire bees' sense of common responsibility.... Although sometimes individual bees fight, basically there is a strong sense of unity and cooperation. We human beings are supposed to be much more advanced, but sometimes we lag behind even small insects.

DALAI LAMA

A man does not
have to be an angel
in order to be a saint.

Albert Schweitzer

348

Saintliness is also
a temptation.

Jean Anouilh

349

Those who know
do not talk.
Those who talk
do not know.

Tao te Ching

350

No suffering befalls
the man who calls
nothing his own.

Dhammapada

351

We find God in
our own being which
is the mirror of God.

Thomas Merton

Holiness comes
by holy deeds,
Not starving flesh
of daily needs.

Shaikh Saadi

The world is not to be put in order, the world is order. It is for us to put ourselves in unison with this order.

HENRY MILLER

It may be agreeable for certain people to live a retired life in a quiet place away from noise and disturbance. But it is certainly more praiseworthy and courageous to practice Buddhism living among your fellow beings, helping them and being of service to them.

WALPOLA SRI RAHULA

Life is what happens
to us while we are
making other plans.

Thomas la Mance

356

Have much and
be confused.

Tao te Ching

I was thrown out of college for cheating on the metaphysics exam; I looked into the soul of the boy next to me.

WOODY ALLEN

Let a Christian follow the precepts of his own faith, let a Hindu and a Jew follow theirs. If they strive long enough, they will ultimately discover God, who runs like a seam under the crusts of rituals and forms.

SWAMI NIKHILANANDA

Having failed to distinguish thoughts from things, we then fail to distinguish words from thoughts. We think that if we can label a thing we have understood it.

MAHA STHAVIRA
SANGHARAKSHITA

To win one hundred victories in one hundred battles is not the highest skill. To subdue the enemy without fighting is the highest skill.

SUN TZU

There ain't no way
to find out why
a snorer can't hear
himself snore.

Mark Twain

362

With them the Seed of Wisdom
    did I sow,
And with my own hand labour'd it to grow:
And this was all the Harvest that I reap'd—
"I came like Water, and like Wind I go."

RUBÁIYÁT
OF OMAR KHAYYÁM

One cannot
invent a religion.

Charles P. Snow

364

E̶very moment of life
is the last, every poem
is a death poem.

Bashō

365

There are two ways of avoiding war:
One is to satisfy everyone's desire, the
other, to content oneself with the good.

UNTO TAHTINEN

From your first day
at school you are
cut off from life to
make theories.

Taisen Deshimaru

367

To understand
everything is to
forgive everything.

Buddha

368

There is nothing either
good or bad, but
thinking makes it so.

William Shakespeare

Hamlet

Mind is the master. What hasn't been created by thought doesn't exist.

Ayya Kemma

Zen teaches nothing; it merely enables us to wake up and become aware. It does not teach, it points.

D. T. SUZUKI

The whole universe
is one commonwealth
of which both gods
and men are members.

Cicero

372

Q: What is the Way and how must it be followed?

A: What sort of *thing* do you suppose the Way to be, that you should wish to *follow* it?

HUANG PO

373

This book was typeset in
Bembo, Evangel, and Gasteur
by Nina Gaskin.

Book design by
Judith Stagnitto Abbate